The Prepper's Guide to All Emergencies

How to Prepare Your Home, Office, & Pets

Jaha Cummings

blue ocean press

Published by:
blue ocean press, an imprint of Aoishima Research Institute
US Office
P.O. Box 510818
Punta Gorda, Florida 33951

Email: books@blueoceanpublications.com
URL: www.PreparedHomeAndOffice.com

ISBN: 978-4-902837-97-1

Photos of assembled kits and supplies are provided courtesy of PreparedHomeAndOffice.com

Table of Contents

To KH

Introduction

This book has been compiled based on my experience in coordinating regional international pandemic planning during the Avian Flu (H5N1), Swine Flu (H1N1), Measles, and Dengue Fever outbreaks between 2008 and 2013; and hurricane and typhoon planning between 2013 and 2020.

This book provides lists of items recommended to be included in emergency survival kits for home, office, school, car, boat, and for pets. Each list is accompanied by a picture of what the contents of a fully assembled kit looks like.

Also included are lists of supplemental items to include in your survival kits for hurricanes, typhoons, and tornados; earthquakes; pandemic flu; emergency hygiene; child safety; and severe weather while on the road.

For those who would like to obtain an assembled kit, kits containing the items listed are available on the website: PreparedHomeAndOffice.com

Be Prepared & Be Safe

Chapter 1
How to Create a Family Emergency Plan

A critical step to preparing for an emergency is to ensure that sure your family has an emergency plan. It is important to plan for the contingency that your family may not be located together when a disaster happens. As such, you need to have a plan in place to determine how your family will get to a safe place, whom each family member will contact, how your family will get back together, and what each person will do in different situations.

This Family Emergency Plan form can be used to organize this information. From this form, you can also create emergency contact cards that you can give to each family member. Adults can keep the cards in their wallet, purse, or briefcase, while your children's contact cards can be placed in their book bags.

Use These 5 Easy Steps to Create Your Family Emergency Plan:

Step 1: Use this form template

This form template (on the following page) can be used to organize your family's emergency plan. It is a good idea to first review the entire form and take an inventory of all the information that you will need to gather to complete it.

Family Emergency Plan Template

Keep a copy of this plan in the emergency survival kit or in a safe place where it can be easily accessed.

After Any Disaster:

1. Turn on a radio and tune into emergency broadcast station.
2. Listen to instructions on locations of emergency centers and how to obtain help.
3. Call your out-of-state contacts.

Emergency Contact Name: _______________ Tel #: ____________

Out-of-Town Contact Name: ____________ Tel #: ____________

Email: _______________________________________

Neighborhood Meeting Place: ___________Tel #: ___________

Regional Meeting Place: ______________Tel #: ___________

Evacuation Location: ________________Tel #: ___________

Fill out the following for each family member and keep it up to date

Name: _________________________ S.S.# _________________

Date of Birth: _________ Medical Info:_______________

Name: _________________________ S.S.# _________________

Date of Birth: _________ Medical Info:_______________

Name: _________________________ S.S.# _________________

Date of Birth: _________ Medical Info:_______________

Name: _________________________ S.S.# _________________

Date of Birth: _________ Medical Info:_______________

Write down where your family spends the most time: work, school, and other places you frequent. Locations such as workplace and school should have site-specific emergency plans that you and your family need to know about.

Work Location One

Address: _______________________

Tel #: _______________________

Evac. Location.: _______________

Work Location Two

Address: _______________________

Tel #: _______________________

Evac. Location.: _______________

Work Location Three

Address: _______________________

Tel #: _______________________

Evac. Location.: _______________

Other Places You Frequent

Address: _______________________

Tel #: _______________________

Evac. Location.: _______________

School Location One

Address: _______________________

Tel #: _______________________

Evac. Location: _______________

School Location Two

Address: _______________________

Tel #: _______________________

Evac. Location: _______________

School Location Three

Address: _______________________

Tel #: _______________________

Evac. Location: _______________

Other Places You Frequent

Address: _______________________

Tel #: _______________________

Evac. Location: _______________

Important Info	*Name*	*Tel #*	*Policy Number*
Doctor			
Doctor			
Other			
Pharmacy			
Medical Insurance			
Homeowner/Rental Insurance			
Veterinarian/Kennel			

Emergency Card Template

(When complete, laminate each card)

FAMILY EMERGENCY PLAN

Emergency Contact Name: ________________________

Telephone #: ________________________

Out-Of-Town Contact Name: ________________________

Telephone #: ________________________

Neighborhood Meeting Place: ________________________

Telephone # ________________________

Other Important Information: ________________________

____

____

DIAL 911 For Emergencies

FAMILY EMERGENCY PLAN

Emergency Contact Name: ________________________

Telephone #: ________________________

Out-Of-Town Contact Name: ________________________

Telephone #: ________________________

Neighborhood Meeting Place: ________________________

Telephone # ________________________

Other Important Information: ________________________

____

____

DIAL 911 For Emergencies

FAMILY EMERGENCY PLAN

Emergency Contact Name: ________________________

Telephone #: ________________________

Out-Of-Town Contact Name: ________________________

Telephone #: ________________________

Neighborhood Meeting Place: ________________________

Telephone # ________________________

Other Important Information: ________________________

____

____

DIAL 911 For Emergencies

Step 2: Organize Your Emergency Contact Network

To complete your family's emergency preparedness plan, you will need to speak to your relatives and friends to identify designated contacts who live out-of-state. These will be people that your household members should notify in case of disaster to let them know they are safe. You want to have out-of-state contacts because phone service in your immediate are may be impacted by the disaster and its aftermath due to high call traffic because. An out-of-town contact may be better positioned to communicate among separated family members.

It is important that each family member knows the phone number of the emergency contact and has a cell phone or phone card to call the emergency contact. Emergency preparedness experts suggest you should have the emergency contact stored in your phone under "ICE" for "in-case-of-emergency." Emergency responders often check for ICE listed under contacts to know whom to contact in case of disaster.

Also, you should teach your family to use text messaging following a disaster. Cell phone networks get jammed up due to high call traffic after a disaster. Text messages, however, use up very little bandwidth from cellular phone networks. Therefore, text messages often avoid any network disruptions making them the most reliable way to reach your emergency contacts with a cell phone.

Step 3: Decide Where You Will Meet

You will also need to identify a neighborhood meeting place which could be your home, a relative's home nearby, or even a close friend's house. Then, you should also decide upon a regional meeting place in case, for example, if your family is spread out across a city when a disaster happens. This can be a landmark or park. You should also have an evacuation location that you are all familiar with in case it is unsafe to meet at any of these other locations. This should generally be somewhere as rural as possible to avoid any hazards.

Step 4: Store Your Preparedness Plan

When you are finished completing the form, store it inside your emergency survival kit that you keep at home. Create emergency contact cards for each family using the information that you included on your preparedness plan.

Step 5: Distribute Emergency Contact Cards

Create the contact cards as described on the template. Handwrite any additional or individual instructions on each card and distribute them to each member of your family. Tell the adults to keep them handy in a wallet, purse, briefcase, etc. For kids, we recommend you stick the cards in their backpacks or book bags.

Chapter 2
Why You Need Emergency Supplies at Home (Office, School, Vehicle, & For Your Pets)

Storing emergency supplies at home, for your home, is an essential part of keeping you and your family safe in times of emergency. After a disaster in your area, you could find yourself without many of the luxuries you are used to. Electricity may be out for weeks leaving you without power and causing water treatment plants to stop working. Your home may suffer structural damage and be unsafe to occupy. You may need to take up shelter outdoors while possibly enduring extreme weather conditions. You or loved ones may suffer injuries and need immediate medical treatment at a time when there might not be medical attention available.

The same applies for offices and schools. A lockdown or stay-in-place scenario could arise that requires you to have to stay at your location until it is safe to leave.

It is also good practice to have an emergency supply kit in your automobile and boat in case a scenario arises where you are stranded for an indeterminate period of time until help can arrive.

Lastly, we cannot neglect to plan for disasters with our pets in mind. They are just as impacted as us by disasters.

Below is a summary of the different categories of emergency preparedness supplies that you should have at home for your family.

Emergency Food

After a large disaster, stores may be closed for several weeks in your area and roads may be unsafe to drive out of your area. That is why it is important to have a supply of emergency food in a 72-hour kit. You should have a minimum of a three-day supply per person but a supply of at least a week is recommended[1]. I recommend that you use US Coast Guard Approved, 5-year shelf-life, 3-day supply of

---

[1] In areas that are prone to hurricanes, typhoons, and tornadoes, it is recommended to have at least 1-2 months of emergency food and water stored on-site, because there may prolonged periods without power or water after a disaster. This additional supply of emergency food and water will also be useful while under stay-at-home orders for disastrous events such as pandemics, chemical accidents, and terrorism.

survival food bars. Some store-bought canned food may only have a 6-month shelf-life.

Emergency Water

After a disaster, running water may be either unsafe to drink or unavailable. Just keeping bottled water at home is not enough. Bottled water only has a 6-month shelf-life; even less if stored in extreme temperatures. It is recommended that at a minimum you have a 3-day supply of drinking water per person in your emergency preparedness kit. However, a survival rule of thumb is that you have a gallon of emergency water per person because you will also need it for sanitation purposes. I recommend that you use US Coast Guard Approved, 5-year shelf-life, 3-day supply of emergency water rations. Since water remains the most important survival item to have, every home survival kit will need to include water purification tablets that can be used along with a 5-gallon container to purify extra water. Storing extra emergency water is recommended as the lists for the survival kits include only a minimum survival supply. The most cost-effective way to store a sufficient amount of emergency water for an entire family is to purchase a 55-gallon water storage barrel and accessories.

Emergency Lights

Because electricity can be out for several weeks after a disaster, you will need emergency lights to navigate through the dark and safely get out of your home in order to travel to a safe location. Each home survival kit list includes essential emergency lights. People often store a regular flashlight and batteries in their emergency preparedness kit, but do not realize that batteries have a shelf-life of 6 months. I have included on the lists a solar and hand crank radio with lantern light which never needs batteries and 12-hour emergency lightsticks that have a 5-year shelf-life. All home kits should also include slow-burning emergency candles and waterproof matches. I also recommend the inclusion of a fluorescent lantern for additional lighting capabilities.

Emergency Radios

In the event of an emergency while you are at home, you will need to know where to go in order to get to a safe location. That is I have included on the lists for emergency preparedness, an emergency radio for listening to emergency broadcasts following a disaster. You should use a solar radio with lantern light which never needs batteries. This emergency radio is highly recommended because regular battery-operated emergency radios have many limitations such as the facts that batteries only last for hours and have an extremely limited shelf-life of around 6 months.

Emergency First Aid Kits

In the event of a disaster or for everyday accidents, emergency first aid kits are always important to have. You probably already have a first aid kit in your home, but individual items likely get taken out of it for occasional injuries. This is why it is important to have a comprehensive first aid kit set aside for emergency preparedness. In addition to the assortment of compresses, antiseptics, bandages, gauze pads and rolls listed in the first aid kit, I also recommend that you include a CPR mask.

Emergency Shelter Supplies

In your emergency preparedness planning, you should consider the fact that your home may be unsafe to occupy. Therefore, you may be forced to stay outdoors for several days if not weeks. That is why you need emergency shelter supplies in your emergency preparedness kit. The lists of the survival kits contain the proper shelter supplies to include space blankets for warmth, ponchos to protect you from the weather, and a tube tent for easy emergency shelter from the elements. Additional emergency home shelter supplies that you can include are a canopy shelter and body warmer pad.

Emergency Search & Rescue Supplies

After a disaster, there is likely to be broken glass and other dangerous items that you will have to deal with when evacuating your home or helping others evacuate. Collapsed structures could trap families in their homes. Therefore, your home emergency preparedness kit should include the emergency search and rescue supplies. An important item, especially for earthquake preparedness, which can save your home and neighborhood, is an emergency gas shut-off wrench. An emergency gas shut-off wrench is included on the lists of the home survival kits along with a swiss army style knife which serves as twelve valuable tools. For setting up camp or shelter, the list also includes nylon cord and duct tape. Each home survival kit should also include leather-palmed work gloves, vinyl gloves, and dust masks for protection from dangerous debris.

Emergency Sanitation Supplies

Plumbing will likely be unavailable after a major disaster. You should remember that you may have to stay outdoors with several other people and neighbors in close proximity. For proper health and sanitation conditions, your emergency survival kit should include emergency sanitation supplies. The 5-gallon container included on the list of the home survival kits is designed to be used as a portable toilet. Each home survival kit should include toilet bags, toilet chemicals, and tissue packs. A toilet seat cover and lid is also recommended.

Chapter 3
Home Survival Kits

Four Person Survival Kit

This is the list for a 4-person, 72-hour survival kit. It is designed to prepare a family of four at home for any disaster. This comprehensive emergency survival kit contains the most effective and reliable emergency preparedness supplies to store at home including food, water, lighting, radio/communication, first-aid, sanitation, and shelter.

The list is as follows:

Food & Water: (4) Food Bars*, (24) Water Pouches*, (50) Water Purification Tablets, (1) Can Opener

Shelter: (4) Emergency Blankets, (4) Ponchos With Hood, (1) Emergency Tent, (1) Plastic Sheeting, (1) Roll Duct Tape

Lighting & Communication: (1) Solar/Hand-Crank Powered Light, Weather Band Radio, & USB Device Charger (this tool is designed to charge smartphones and other USB devices so you can stay in touch with family in the event of a disaster, and never needs batteries), (4) Out-of-State Contact Card, (2) Green Lightsticks, (1) Yellow Lightstick, (5) Emergency Candles, (40) Waterproof Matches

First Aid: (1) Medium Sized First Aid Kit, (200) Potassium Iodate Pills

Search & Rescue: (1) Safety Whistle, (4) Dust Masks, (1) Pair Vinyl Gloves, (1) Pair Work Gloves, (1) Swiss Army Style Knife, (1) Multi-function Utility Tool, (1) Nylon Utility Cord

Sanitation: (12) Sanitation/Toilet Bags, (1) Package Toilet Chemicals, (4) Tissue Packs, (1) Snap-on Toilet Seat

These supplies should be stored in a 5 Gallon Bucket Container.

*It is recommended that your kit contain US Coast Guard Approved Food and Water with a 5-Year Shelf-Life.

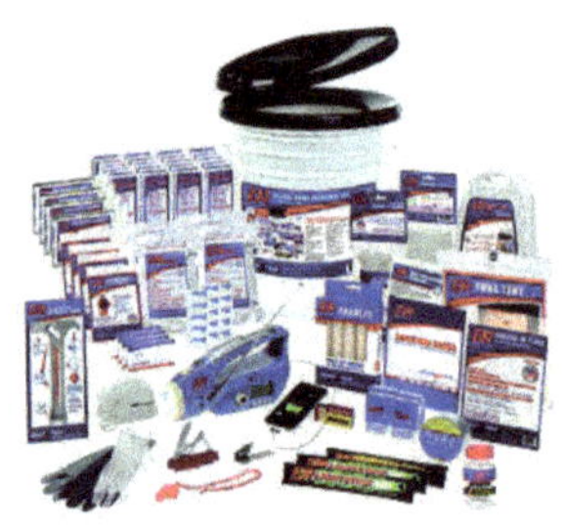

Pictured: 4 Person Survival Kit

Two Person Survival Kit

This is the list for a 2-person, 72-hour survival kit. It is designed to prepare a small home or apartment for any disaster. This comprehensive emergency survival kit contains the most effective and reliable emergency preparedness supplies to store at home including food, water, lighting, radio/communication, first-aid, sanitation, and shelter.

The list is as follows:

Food & Water. (2) Food Bars*, (12) Water Pouches*, (50) Water Purification Tablets, (1) Can Opener

Shelter. (2) Emergency Blankets, (2) Ponchos With Hood, (1) Emergency Tent, (1) Plastic Sheeting, (1) Roll Duct Tape, (1) Solar / Hand-Crank Powered Light, Weather Band Radio, & USB Device Charger

Lighting & Communication. (2) Out-of-State Contact Card, (1) Green Lightsticks, (1) Yellow Lightstick, (5) Emergency Candles, (40) Waterproof Matches

First Aid. (1) Medium Sized First Aid Kit, (200) Potassium Iodate Pills

Search & Rescue: (1) Safety Whistle, (2) Dust Masks, (1) Pair Vinyl Gloves, (1) Pair Work Gloves, (1) Swiss Army Style Knife, (1) Multi-function Utility Tool, (1) Nylon Utility Cord, (1) Survival Guide

Sanitation: (1) Snap-on Toilet Seat (optional), (12) Sanitation/Toilet Bags, (1) Package Toilet Chemicals, (2) Tissue Packs

These supplies should be stored in a 5 Gallon Bucket Container.

*It is recommended that your kit contain US Coast Guard Approved Food and Water with a 5-Year Shelf-Life.

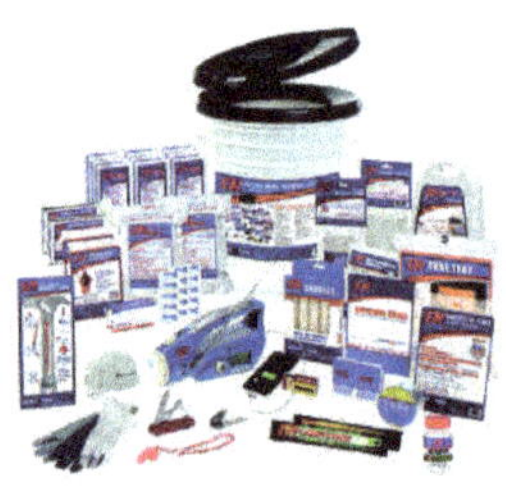

Pictured: 2 Person Survival Kit

Backpack Survival Kit

This is the list for a backpack survival kit that contains the most effective and reliable survival food, water, lighting, radio/communication, first-aid, sanitation, and shelter supplies to be prepared for all disasters.

The list as is follows:

Food & Water: (4) Food Bars*, (24) Water Pouches*, (50) Water Purification Tablets

Shelter: (5) Emergency Blankets, (5) Ponchos With Hood

Lighting & Communication: (1) Solar/Hand-Crank Powered Light, Weather Band Radio, & USB Device Charger, (2) Green Lightsticks, (1) Yellow Lightstick, (5) Emergency Candles, (40) Waterproof Matches

First Aid: (1) OSHA First Aid Kit, (200) Potassium Iodate Pills

Search & Rescue: (1) Safety Whistle, (5) Dust Masks, (1) Pair Vinyl Gloves, (1) Pair Work Gloves, (1) Pry Crow Bar 15"

Sanitation: (5) Tissue packs

These supplies should be stored in a Backpack.

*It is recommended that your kit contain US Coast Guard Approved Food and Water with a 5-Year Shelf-Life.

Pictured: Backpack Survival Kit

Chapter 4
Office Survival Kits

Ensure that your employees are safe after a disaster. These lists include the most critical and reliable supplies to evacuate or shelter-in-place at the office.

5 Person Office Survival Kit

This is the list for a 5-person, 72-hour survival kit designed for a small office to contain the most effective and reliable survival food, water, lighting, radio/communication, first-aid, sanitation, and shelter supplies to prepare for all disasters.

The list is as follows:

Food & Water: (5) Food Bars*, (30) Water Pouches*, (50) Water Purification Tablets

Shelter: (5) Emergency Blankets, (1) Tent

Lighting & Communication: (1) Solar / Hand-Crank Powered Light, Weather Band Radio, & USB Device Charger (this tool is designed to charge smartphones and other USB devices so you can stay in touch with family in the event of a disaster, and never needs batteries), (2) Green Lightsticks, (1) Yellow Lightstick, (5) Emergency Candles, (40) Waterproof Matches

First Aid: (1) OSHA First Aid Kit, (200) Potassium Iodate Pills

Search & Rescue: (1) Safety Whistle, (5) Dust Masks, (2) Pair Vinyl Gloves, (1) Pair Work Gloves

Sanitation: (1) Snap-on Toilet Seat, (12) Sanitation/Toilet Bags, (1) Package Toilet Chemicals, (5) Tissue packs

These supplies should be kept in a 5 Gallon Bucket Container.

*It is recommended that your kit contain US Coast Guard Approved Food and Water with a 5-Year Shelf-Life.

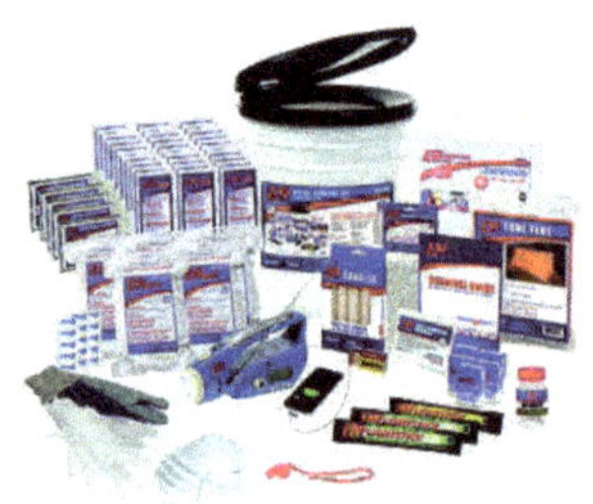

Pictured: 5 Person Office Survival Kit

10 Person Office Survival Kit

This is the list for a 10-person, 72-hour survival kit is designed to contain the most effective and reliable survival food, water, lighting, radio/communication, first-aid, sanitation, and shelter supplies to prepare a small office for all disasters.

The list is as follows:

Food & Water: (10) Food Bars*, (60) Water Pouches*, (50) Water Purification Tablets

Shelter: (10) Emergency Blankets, (1) Tent, (1) Plastic Sheeting, (1) Roll Duct Tape

Lighting & Communication: (1) Solar / Hand-Crank Powered Light, Weather Band Radio, & USB Device Charger, (2) Green Lightsticks, (1) Yellow Lightstick, (5) Emergency Candles, (40) Waterproof Matches

First Aid: (1) OSHA First Aid Kit, (200) Potassium Iodate Pills

Search & Rescue: (1) Safety Whistle, (10) Dust Masks, (2) Pair Vinyl Gloves, (1) Pair Work Gloves, (1) Pry/Crow Bar 15"

Sanitation: (1) Snap-on Toilet Seat, (12) Sanitation/Toilet Bags, (1) Package Toilet Chemicals, (10) Tissue packs

These supplies should be stored in a 5 Gallon Bucket Container.

*It is recommended that your kit contain US Coast Guard Approved Food and Water with a 5-Year Shelf-Life.

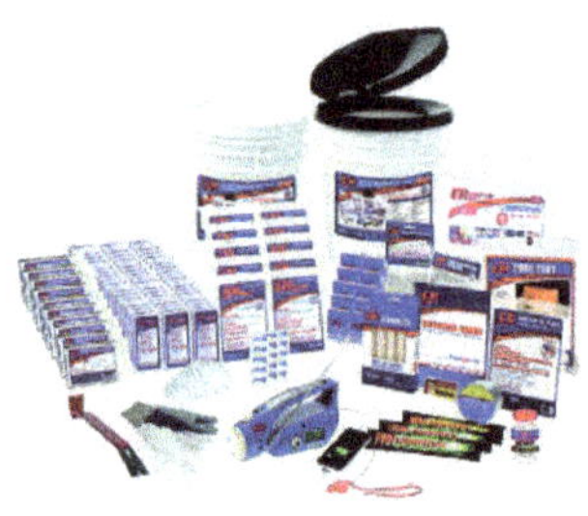

Pictured: 10 Person Ultimate Survival Kit

20 Person Office Survival Kit

This is the list for a 20-person, 72-hour survival kit is designed to contain the most effective and reliable survival food, water, lighting, radio/communication, first-aid, sanitation, and shelter supplies to prepare a medium-sized office for all disasters.

The list is as follows:

Food & Water: (20) Food Bars*, (120) Water Pouches*, (50) Water Purification Tablets

Shelter: (20) Emergency Blankets, (1) Tent, (1) Plastic Sheeting, (1) Roll Duct Tape

Lighting & Radios: (1) Solar / Hand-Crank Powered Light, Weather Band Radio, & USB Device Charger, (3) Green Lightsticks, (1) Yellow Lightstick, (5) Emergency Candles, (40) Waterproof Matches

First Aid: (1) OSHA First Aid Kit, (200) Potassium Iodate Pills

Search & Rescue: (1) Safety Whistle, (20) Dust Masks, (2) Pair Vinyl Gloves, (1) Pair Work Gloves, (1) Pry/Crow Bar 15"

Sanitation: (1) Snap-on Toilet Seat, (12) Sanitation/Toilet Bags, (1) Package Toilet Chemicals, (20) Tissue packs

These supplies should be stored in a 5 Gallon Bucket Container.

*It is recommended that your kit contain US Coast Guard Approved Food and Water with a 5-Year Shelf-Life.

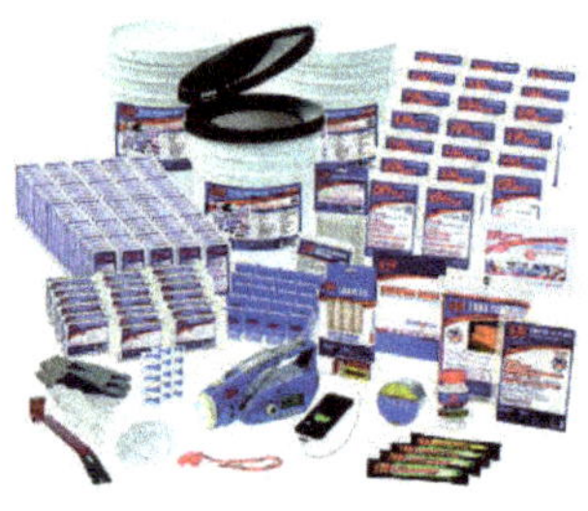

Pictured: 20 Person Ultimate Survival Kit

100 Person Ultimate Survival Kit

This is the list for a 100-person, 72-hour survival kit designed to contain the most effective and reliable survival food, water, lighting, radio/communication, first-aid, sanitation, and shelter supplies to prepare a large office for all disasters.

The list is as follows:

Food & Water: (100) Food Bars*, (600) Water Pouches*, (250) Water Purification Tablets

Shelter: (100) Emergency Blankets, (5) Tent, (5) Plastic Sheeting, (5) Roll Duct Tape

Lighting & Communication: (1) Solar / Hand-Crank Powered Light, Weather Band Radio, & USB Device Charger, (15) Green Lightsticks, (5) Yellow Lightsticks, (25) Emergency Candles, (200) Waterproof Matches

First Aid: (5) OSHA First Aid Kit, (200) Potassium Iodate Pills

Search & Rescue: (5) Safety Whistle, (100) Dust Masks, (10) Pair Vinyl Gloves, (5) Pair Work Gloves, (5) Pry/Crow Bar 15"

Sanitation: (5) Snap-on Toilet Seat, (12) Sanitation/Toilet Bags, (5) Package Toilet Chemicals, (100) Tissue packs

These supplies should be stored in a 5 Gallon Bucket Container.

*It is recommended that your kit contain US Coast Guard Approved Food and Water with a 5-Year Shelf-Life.

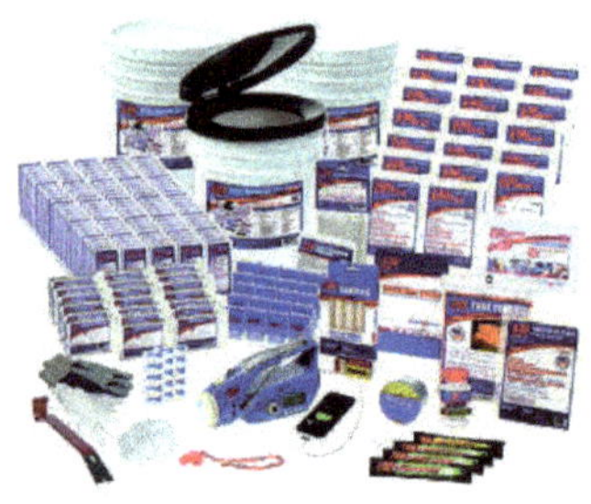

Pictured: 100 Person Office Survival Kit

1 Person Lunchbox Survival Kit

This is the list for a 1-person, 72-hour survival kit is packaged in a lunchbox style container. This survival kit contains the basic emergency preparedness supplies to prepare for all disasters including emergency food, water, shelter, light, first aid, and sanitation.

This list as is follows:

Food & Water: (1) Food Bar*, (6) Water Pouches*

Shelter: (1) Emergency Blanket

Lighting & Communication: (1) Green Lightstick

First Aid: (1) Personal First Aid Kit, (1) Dust Mask, (1) Pair Vinyl Gloves, (1) Tissue pack

These supplies should be stored in a Lunchbox Style Container.

*It is recommended that your kit contain US Coast Guard Approved Food and Water with a 5-Year Shelf-Life.

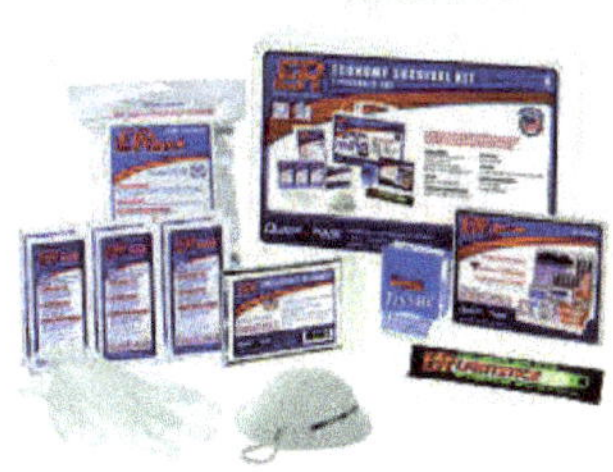

Pictured: 1 Person Lunchbox Survival Kit

1 Person Bagged Survival Kit

This is the list for a 1-person, 72-hour survival kit is packaged in a gallon size zip-lock bag. This emergency survival kit contains the most effective emergency supplies for emergency preparedness including the emergency food, water, and shelter supplies to prepare for all disasters.

The list as is follows:

Food & Water: (1) Food Bar*, (6) Water Pouches*

Shelter: (1) Emergency Blanket

These supplies should be stored in a Gallon-sized Plastic Zip-Lock bag.

*It is recommended that your kit contain US Coast Guard Approved Food and Water with a 5-Year Shelf-Life.

Pictured: 1 Person Bagged Survival Kit

Backpack Survival Kit

This is the list for a backpack survival kit that contains the most effective and reliable survival food, water, lighting, radio/communication, first-aid, sanitation, and shelter supplies to be prepared for all disasters.

The list as is follows:

Food & Water: (4) Food Bars*, (24) Water Pouches*, (50) Water Purification Tablets

Shelter: (5) Emergency Blankets, (5) Ponchos With Hood

Lighting & Communication: (1) Solar/Hand-Crank Powered Light, Weather Band Radio, & USB Device Charger, (2) Green Lightsticks, (1) Yellow Lightstick, (5) Emergency Candles, (40) Waterproof Matches

First Aid: (1) OSHA First Aid Kit, (200) Potassium Iodate Pills

Search & Rescue: (1) Safety Whistle, (5) Dust Masks, (1) Pair Vinyl Gloves, (1) Pair Work Gloves, (1) Pry Crow Bar 15"

Sanitation: (5) Tissue packs

These supplies should be stored in a Backpack.

*It is recommended that your kit contain US Coast Guard Approved Food and Water with a 5-Year Shelf-Life.

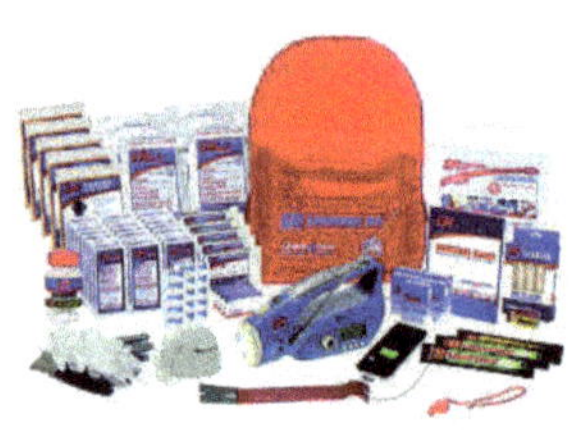

Pictured: Backpack Survival Kit

Lockdown Survival Kit

This is the list for a survival kit designed for offices and classrooms with all the necessary emergency supplies to prepare for any disaster. This comprehensive emergency survival kit contains the most effective emergency supplies for emergency preparedness including the emergency food, water, lighting, radio, first-aid, sanitation, and shelter supplies to prepare for all disasters.

The list is as follows:

Food & Water: (4) Food Bars, (24) Water Pouches, (50) Water Purification Tablets

Shelter: (5) Emergency Blankets, (1) Plastic Sheeting, (1) Roll Duct Tape

Lighting & Communication: (1) Solar/Hand-Crank Powered Light, Weather Band Radio, & USB Device Charger, (2) Green Lightsticks, (1) Yellow Lightstick, (5) Emergency Candles, (40) Waterproof Matches

First Aid: (1) OSHA First Aid Kit, (200) Potassium Iodate Pills

Search & Rescue: (1) Safety Whistle, (5) Dust Masks, (2) Pair Vinyl Gloves, (1) Pair Work Gloves, (1) Pry/Crow Bar 15"

Sanitation: (1) Snap-on Toilet Seat, (12) Sanitation/Toilet Bags, (1) Package Toilet Chemicals, (5) Tissue packs

These supplies should be stored in a 5 Gallon Bucket Container.

*It is recommended that your kit contain US Coast Guard Approved Food and Water with a 5-Year Shelf-Life.

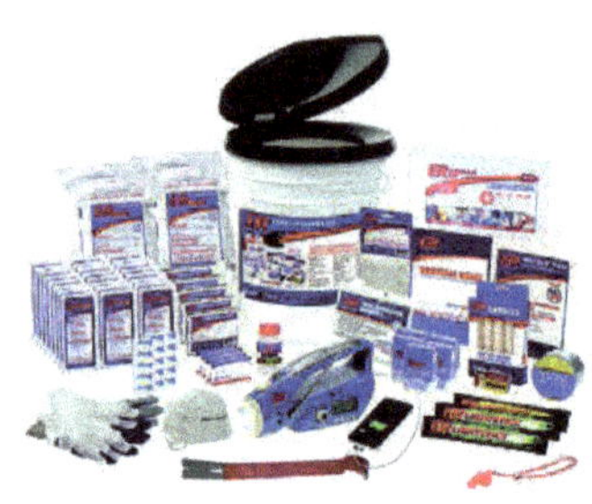

Pictured: Lockdown Survival Kit

Chapter 5
School Survival Kits

Is your school prepared for a disaster? School kits need to include the most critical and reliable supplies.

1 Person Lunchbox Survival Kit

This is the list for a 1-person, 72-hour survival kit is packaged in a lunchbox style container. This survival kit contains the basic emergency preparedness supplies to prepare for all disasters including emergency food, water, shelter, light, first aid, and sanitation.

This list as is follows:

Food & Water: (1) Food Bar*, (6) Water Pouches*

Shelter: (1) Emergency Blanket

Lighting & Communication: (1) Green Lightstick

First Aid: (1) Personal First Aid Kit, (1) Dust Mask, (1) Pair Vinyl Gloves, (1) Tissue pack

These supplies should be stored in a Lunchbox Style Container.

*It is recommended that your kit contain US Coast Guard

Approved Food and Water with a 5-Year Shelf-Life.

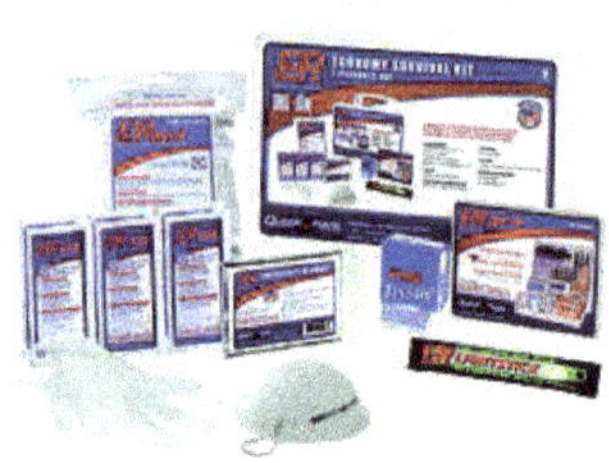

Pictured: 1 Person Lunchbox Survival Kit

1 Person Bagged Survival Kit

This is the list for a 1-person, 72-hour survival kit is packaged in a gallon size zip-lock bag. This emergency survival kit contains the most effective emergency supplies for emergency preparedness including the emergency food, water, and shelter supplies to prepare for all disasters.

The list as is follows:

Food & Water: (1) Food Bar*, (6) Water Pouches*

Shelter: (1) Emergency Blanket

These supplies should be stored in a Gallon-sized Plastic Zip-Lock bag.

*It is recommended that your kit contain US Coast Guard Approved Food and Water with a 5-Year Shelf-Life.

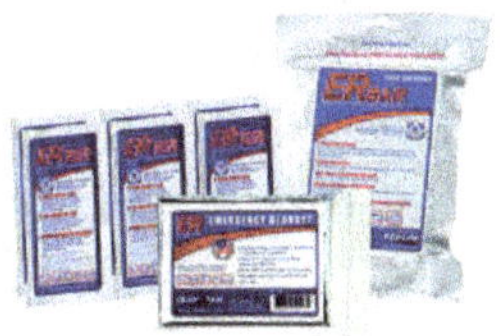

Pictured: 1 Person Bagged Survival Kit

Backpack Survival Kit

This is the list for a backpack survival kit that contains the most effective and reliable survival food, water, lighting, radio/communication, first-aid, sanitation, and shelter supplies to be prepared for all disasters.

The list as is follows:

Food & Water: (4) Food Bars*, (24) Water Pouches*, (50) Water Purification Tablets

Shelter: (5) Emergency Blankets, (5) Ponchos With Hood

Lighting & Communication: (1) Solar/Hand-Crank Powered Light, Weather Band Radio, & USB Device Charger, (2) Green Lightsticks, (1) Yellow Lightstick, (5) Emergency Candles, (40) Waterproof Matches

First Aid: (1) OSHA First Aid Kit, (200) Potassium Iodate Pills

Search & Rescue: (1) Safety Whistle, (5) Dust Masks, (1) Pair Vinyl Gloves, (1) Pair Work Gloves, (1) Pry Crow Bar 15"

Sanitation: (5) Tissue packs

These supplies should be stored in a Backpack.

*It is recommended that your kit contain US Coast Guard Approved Food and Water with a 5-Year Shelf-Life.

Pictured: Backpack Survival Kit

Lockdown Survival Kit

This is the list for a survival kit designed for offices and classrooms with all the necessary emergency supplies to prepare for any disaster. This comprehensive emergency survival kit contains the most effective emergency supplies for emergency preparedness including the emergency food, water, lighting, radio, first-aid, sanitation, and shelter supplies to prepare an office for all disasters.

The list is as follows:

Food & Water: (4) Food Bars, (24) Water Pouches, (50) Water Purification Tablets

Shelter: (5) Emergency Blankets, (1) Plastic Sheeting, (1) Roll Duct Tape

Lighting & Communication: (1) Solar/Hand-Crank Powered Light, Weather Band Radio, & USB Device Charger, (2) Green Lightsticks, (1) Yellow Lightstick, (5) Emergency Candles, (40) Waterproof Matches

First Aid: (1) OSHA First Aid Kit, (200) Potassium Iodate Pills

Search & Rescue: (1) Safety Whistle, (5) Dust Masks, (2) Pair Vinyl Gloves, (1) Pair Work Gloves, (1) Pry/Crow Bar 15"

Sanitation: (1) Snap-on Toilet Seat, (12) Sanitation/Toilet Bags, (1) Package Toilet Chemicals, (5) Tissue packs

These supplies should be stored in a 5 Gallon Bucket Container.

*It is recommended that your kit contain US Coast Guard Approved Food and Water with a 5-Year Shelf-Life.

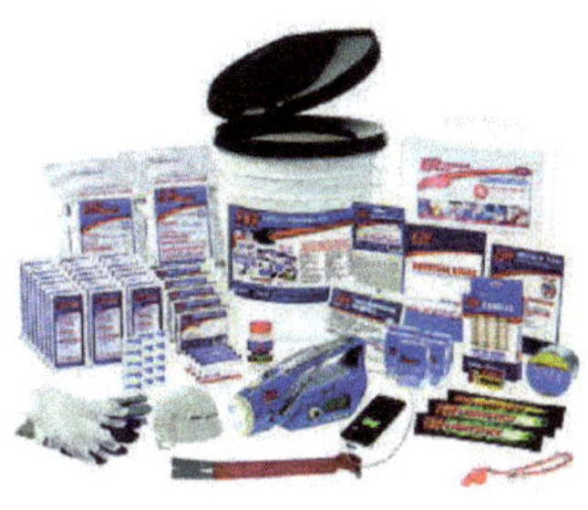

Pictured: Lockdown Survival Kit

Chapter 6
Pet Survival Kits

Are your pets and service animals prepared for a disaster?

Dog Survival Kit

This is the list for an emergency dog survival kit. It contains emergency supplies for up to two dogs. This pet survival kit contains the most effective supplies for emergency preparedness including the emergency food, water, lighting, first-aid, sanitation, and shelter supplies to prepare your pets.

This is list is as follows:

(2) Dog Food Packets*
(12) Water Pouches
(2) Thermal Blankets
(2) Emergency Lightsticks
(50) Water Purification Tablets
(1) Deluxe Pet First Aid Kit
(2) Bowls
(2) Leads - Collar & Leash
(12) Sanitation/Poop Bags
(2) Dog Toys
(1) Rope
(1) Decal

These supplies should be stored in a durable Nylon Bag.

* It is recommended that the dog food be vacuum sealed with a 5-year shelf life.

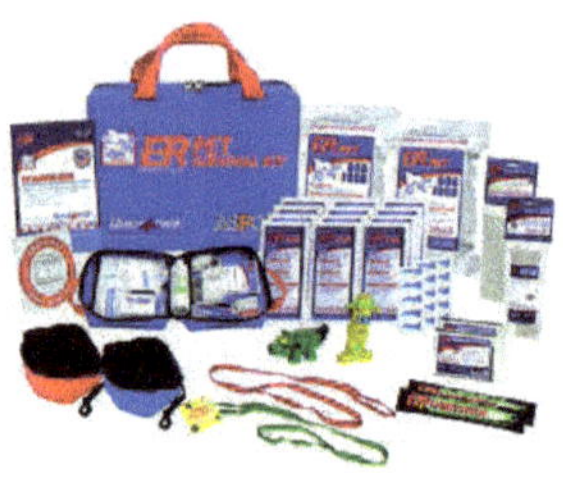

Pictured: Dog Survival Kit

Cat Survival Kit

This is the list for an emergency cat survival kit that contains emergency supplies for up to two cats. This pet survival kit contains the most effective supplies for emergency preparedness including the emergency food, water, lighting, first-aid, sanitation, and shelter supplies to prepare your cats.

The list as is follows:
(2) Cat Food Packets
(12) Water Pouches
(2) Thermal Blankets
(2) Emergency Lightsticks
(50) Water Purification Tablets
(1) Deluxe Pet First Aid Kit
(2) Bowls
(2) Leads - Collar & Leash
(12) Sanitation/Poop Bags
(2) Cat Toys
(1) Rope
(1) Decal
(1) Decal

These supplies should be stored in a durable Nylon Bag.

* It is recommended that the cat food be vacuum sealed with a 5-year shelf life.

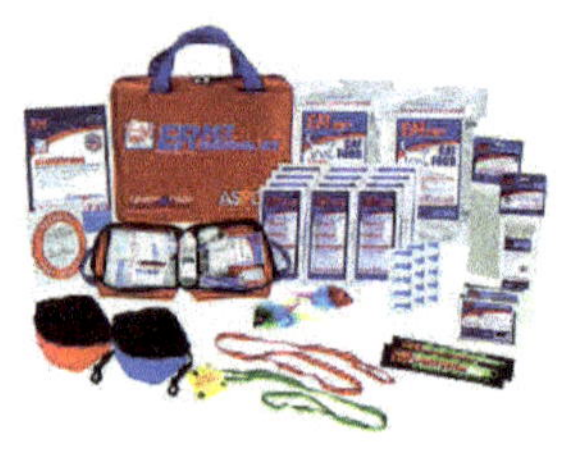

Pictured: Cat Survival Kit

Chapter 7
Automobile/Boat Kits

In addition to the roadside and severe weather kit lists that are included in this chapter, it is good practice to keep a survival kit inside your automobile and boat, so that you are prepared when the unexpected occurs. I have provided lists for a Backpack Survival Kit that is easy to store in an automobile or boat and can be used as your as Automobile or Boat Survival Kit.

Roadside and Severe Weather Kit

This is the list for a roadside severe weather kit. This kit is designed as an accessory to your Automobile Survival Kit. This kit contains the additional emergency tools and supplies you will need to get you back on the road while safely enduring severe weather conditions.

This list is as follows:

(1) Insulated Jumper Cables
(1) Flat Head Screwdriver
(1) Phillips Head Screwdriver
(1) Tire Pressure Gauge
(1) 10 piece Nut Driver Set
(1) Slip Joint Pliers
(1) Cloth Work Gloves
(1) Electrical Tape
(12) Assorted Electric Terminals and Fuses - Packaged in a

convenient, hard shell carrying case with handle

(1) Collapsible Safety Hazard Cone - Bright florescent orange reflector, LED strobe blinker light, and supply of batteries.

(1) Warning Reflective Triangle

(1) Heavy Duty Tow Rope - 4500 lbs towing capacity

(1) Tire Puncture Repair Kit

(1) Accident Report Form with Pencil

(1) Auto Emergency Safety Hammer - Nickel-plated dual hammer tip, seat belt cutter, built in flashlight, blinking LED strobe light, glow in the dark indicator, and supply of batteries.

(1) Folding Shovel

(1) 12-hour Green Lightstick with 5 year shelf-life

(1) 12-hour Yellow Lightstick with 5 year shelf-life

(1) Body Warmer Pads that can provide instant heat for over 12 hours

(1) Hand Warmer Pads that can provide instant heat for over 12 hours

(1) Ice Scraper

(1) Safety Vest

(1) Utility Knife

Keep these supplies in a Durable Duffle Bag.

Pictured: Roadside and Severe Weather Kit

Roadside Kit

This is the list of a kit that you can use to be prepared for an automotive emergency. This kit is an accessory to your Automobile Survival Kit. This kit contains the additional emergency tools and supplies you will need to get you back on the road safely.

The list is as follows:

Insulated Jumper Cables
Flat Head Screwdriver
Phillips Head Screwdriver
Tire Pressure Gauge
10-piece nut driver set
Slip Joint Pliers
Cloth Work Gloves
Electrical Tape
12 assorted Electric Terminals and Fuses

This kit should be stored in a hard shell carrying case.

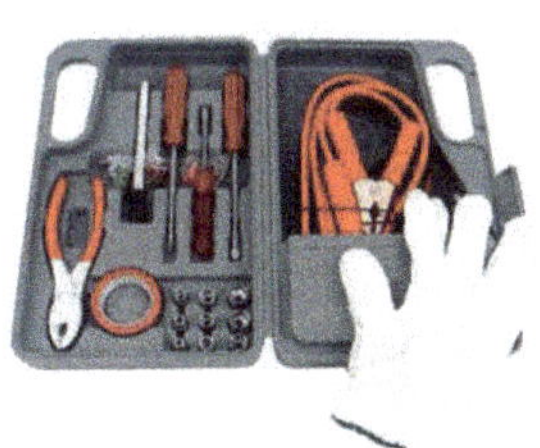

Pictured: Roadside Kit

Backpack Survival Kit (to be used an Automobile or Boat Survival Kit)

This is the list for a backpack survival kit that contains the most effective and reliable survival food, water, lighting, radio/communication, first-aid, sanitation, and shelter supplies to be prepared for all disasters.

The list as is follows:

Food & Water: (4) Food Bars*, (24) Water Pouches*, (50) Water Purification Tablets

Shelter: (5) Emergency Blankets, (5) Ponchos With Hood

Lighting & Communication: (1) Solar/Hand-Crank Powered Light, Weather Band Radio, & USB Device Charger, (2) Green Lightsticks, (1) Yellow Lightstick, (5) Emergency Candles, (40) Waterproof Matches

First Aid: (1) OSHA First Aid Kit, (200) Potassium Iodate Pills

Search & Rescue: (1) Safety Whistle, (5) Dust Masks, (1) Pair Vinyl Gloves, (1) Pair Work Gloves, (1) Pry Crow Bar 15"

Sanitation: (5) Tissue packs

These supplies should be stored in a Backpack.

*It is recommended that your kit contain US Coast Guard

Approved Food and Water with a 5-Year Shelf-Life.

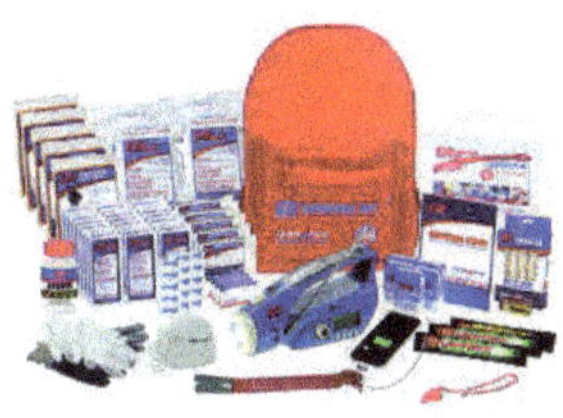

Pictured: Backpack Survival Kit

Chapter 8
Emergency Kits

These are the lists for kits that contain additional supplies to prepare for specific disasters. These lists are designed to supplement your Home, Office, School, or Pet Survival Kits.

Basic Pandemic Flu Kit

Your emergency pandemic flu kit should contain the basic supplies for protection from the spread of the pandemic flu as recommended by the U.S. Centers of Disease Control and World Health Organization to prevent a pandemic flu virus.

The list is as follows:

(1) N95 Particulate Respirator
(4) Antimicrobial Wipes - Disinfectant wipes prevent spread of germs and maintain sanitary conditions.
(1) Pair of Nitrile Gloves Large - 5 mil. thick industrial grade.
(1) Antiseptic Hand Sanitizer Gel - 4 oz.

Keep these supplies in a Gallon-sized Zip-lock Bag.

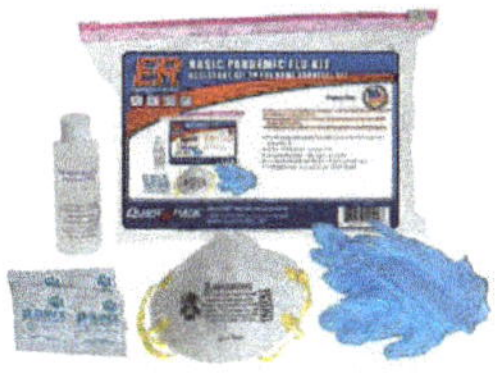

Pictured: Basic Pandemic Flu Kit

Comprehensive Pandemic Flu Kit

This is a list of supplies to supplement your Office/Home Survival Kit to contain the most effective supplies for protection from the spread of the pandemic flu, as recommended by the U.S. Centers of Disease Control and World Health Organization to prevent a pandemic flu virus.

The list is as follows:

(1) Tyvek Suit - DuPont hooded coveralls with elastic wrists, ankles, and nonskid socks.
(1) Safety Goggles - Eye shield protection. Adjustable head band.
(4) N95 Particulate Respirator.
(1) Liquid Bandage Spray - 3 oz.
(12) Antimicrobial Wipes.
(2) Tissue Packs - Multi-task sheets.
(2) Pair of Nitrile Gloves - 5 mil. thick industrial grade.
(2) Biohazard Bags - For sanitary disposal.
(1) Antiseptic Hand Sanitizer Gel - 4 oz.
(1) Plastic Sheeting - Shelter-in-place for protection from contaminants.
(1) Roll of Duct Tape - For use with plastic sheeting.

Keep these supplies in a Waterproof Container.

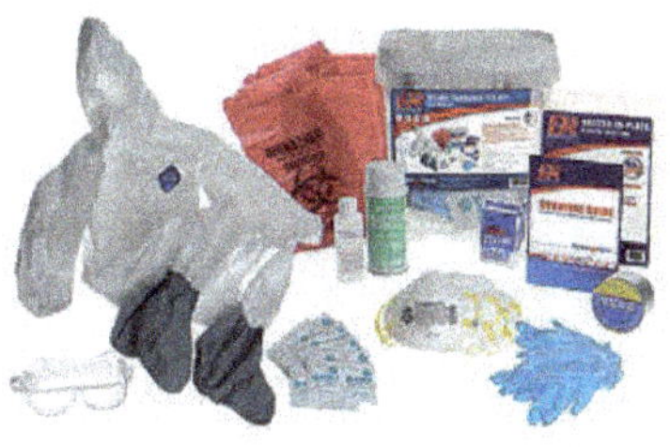

Pictured: Comprehensive Pandemic Flu Kit

Earthquake Kit

This is a list of supplies to supplement your Office or Home Survival Kit with additional emergency supplies specifically designed to prepare you for earthquakes. This kit is specially designed to contain the most effective supplies to help protect your home and protect against damage or injury that may occur during an accident or earthquake.

The list is as follows:

(1) Package Picture Hooks - No-fall picture hooks. Support and protect even large pictures or frames.
(1) Jar of Museum/Quake Wax - Safely anchors artifacts. Nontoxic formula is effective and easy to use.
(2) Pairs Furniture Fastening Straps - Anchor heavy furniture. Furniture can shift and block your exit.
(1) Power Failure Light - Rechargeable automatic light. Automatically lights up when power goes out.
(1) Set of Safety Adhesive Fasteners - Safely anchor appliances.

Keep these supplies in a Waterproof Container.

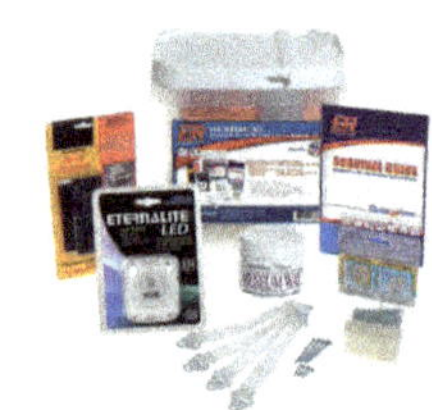

Pictured: Earthquake Kit

Hurricane/Typhoon Kit

This is a list of supplies to supplement your Office or Home Survival Kit with additional emergency supplies specifically designed to prepare your office or home for hurricanes and typhoons.

The list is as follows:

(1) Duct Tape - Endless applications. An essential for any kit.
(1) Tarp - 10' x 12' reinforced rip stop polyethylene. Great for quick, on the spot shelter.
(1) Shelter-In-Place Plastic Sheeting
(5) Emergency Candles
(1) Box of Waterproof Matches
(1) N95 Particulate Respirator
(1) Axe - Flattened head for hammering. 2 tools in 1
(3) Document Storage Bags – These need to be waterproof, zip-lock bags. These are to protect important documents, IDs, and more.
(1) Safety Goggles - Protect eyes from harmful dust and debris which might arise.
(1) Folding Shovel
(1) Fold A Stove – One that is compact and ignites easily.

Keep these supplies in a Waterproof Container.

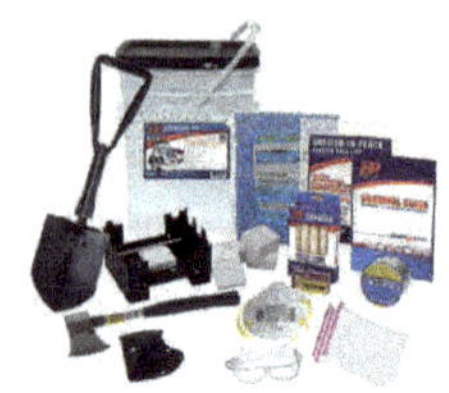

Pictured: Hurricane/Typhoon Kit

Hygiene Kit

This is a list of supplies to supplement your Office or Home Survival Kit specifically designed for family hygiene following a disaster. This list contains the personal hygiene supplies needed to maintain healthy, sanitary conditions for you and your family following a disaster.

The list is as follows:

(1) Antibacterial Hand Sanitizer
(12) Antimicrobial Wipes
(4) Personal Hygiene Kits - 4 toothbrushes/pastes, 4 combs, 4 bio-hazard bag, 12 wet-wipes, 4 razors, 4 tissue packs, 4 sanitary napkins. Complete set of comprehensive supplies.
(1) Roll of Toilet Paper
(1) ReadyBath - 8 rinse-free; hypoallergenic total body-cleansing system wipes.
(1) Shampoo & Body Wash - 8 oz. PH balanced no-rinse cleansing system spray bottle.
(1) Spray Bottle Insect Repellent - With DEET.
(10) Sunscreen Lotion Packets - SPF 30+ protects skin.
(12) Sanitation/Toilet Bags - For use with container as a portable toilet.
(1) Package Toilet Chemicals - Maintain sanitary conditions by using with container, seat, and bags.

Keep these supplies in a Waterproof Container.

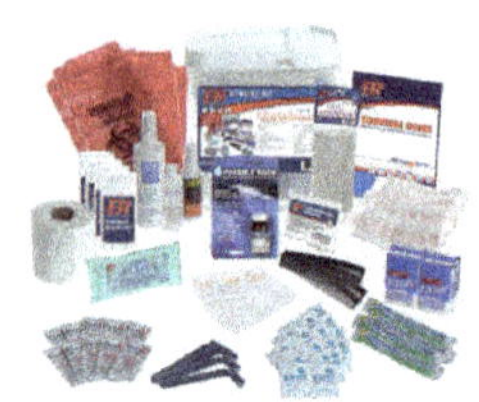

Pictured: Hygiene Kit

Child Safety Kit

This is a list of supplies to supplement your Office or Home Survival Kit specifically designed for child safety. This kit is designed to protect your child from many of the common, everyday dangers that lay in the office or home or from any number of dangers outside of the office or home.

The list is as follows:

(1) Child ID & Records Kit
(12) Outlet Safety Plugs
(3) Doorknob Grips
(4) Safety Corner Bumpers
(7) Child Safety Cabinet Latches
(1) All Purpose Safety Strap - Keep kids out of dangerous area.
(1) Automatic Night Light - Night light and power failure light in one. Provides light during a power outage.
(2) Pairs of Furniture Fastening Straps - Safely anchor furniture. Arrange as desired to prevent accidents.

Keep these supplies in Waterproof Container.

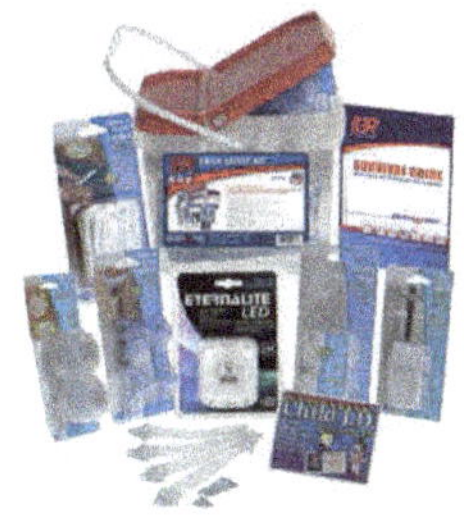

Picture: Child Safety Kit

Chapter 9
Hurricane, Typhoon, and Tornado Survival Kit

Be ready for hurricanes, typhoons, and tornados.

Hurricane/Typhoon/Tornado Survival Kit

This 2 Person Hurricane/Typhoon/Tornado Survival Kit contains essential, lifesaving items necessary to sustain two individuals for three days in the event of a quick home evacuation or the need to shelter-in-place following a devastating hurricane, typhoon, or tornado. When packaged in a portable, water-resistant 5 or 6-gallon container, this kit offers several strategic emergency preparedness advantages.

The list is as follows:

Food & Water: (2) Food Bars*, (12) Emergency Water Pouches*, (1) Aquatabs® Water Purification Tablets
Lighting & Radios: (1) Solar/Hand-Crank Powered Flashlight and Weather Band Radio, (2) Green Lightsticks, (5) Emergency Candles, (1) Box of 40 Waterproof Matches
First Aid: (1) Medium Sized First Aid Kit
Shelter: (2) Emergency Blankets, (2) Emergency Ponchos, (1) Tarp - 10' x 12' reinforced rip stop polyethylene
Sanitation/Hygiene: (1) Packaged in 5 or 6 gallon Bucket

container with toilet top lid, (12) Sanitation/Toilet Bags, (1) Package Toilet Chemicals, (1) Personal Hygiene Kit – 2 toothbrushes/pastes, 1 comb, 3 wet-wipes, 1 razor, 1 tissue pack, 1 sanitary napkin, (18) sunscreen packs, (1) Insect repellent

Search & Rescue: (1) 50 ft. Nylon Cord, (1) Duct Tape, (1) Multi-Purpose tool, (1) Pry bar, (2) N95 Particulate Respirator, (2) Work Gloves, (2) Safety Goggles, (1) Folding Shovel

Other: (1) Document Storage Bags - Waterproof, zip-lock bags, (1) CPR, AED and Basic First Aid Reference Guide

These supplies should be stored in a 5- or 6-Gallon Bucket Container.

*It is recommended that your kit contain US Coast Guard Approved Food and Water with a 5-Year Shelf-Life.

Pictured: Hurricane/Typhoon/Tornado Kit

Chapter 10
Emergency First Aid Kits

Always have first aid supplies on hand.

25 Person First Aid Kit

This is a list for a First Aid Kit is designed to provide basic first aid for offices or groups of up to 25 people.

The list as is follows:

References: (1) first aid guide

Instruments: (1) scissors, (1) tweezer, (4) vinyl gloves, (1) CPR Breathing Barrier

Injury Treatment: (1) instant cold compress, (1) triangular bandage, (1) 1/2" x 5 yds. roll adhesive tape

Bandages: (50) 1" x 3" adhesive plastic, (25) Adhesive Spot Bandages, 7/8" x 7/8", (1) Butterfly Wound Closures, (2) 2" x 4.1 yd. conforming gauze roll, (1) 3" x 4.1 yd. conforming gauze roll, (1) knuckle fabric, (1) fingertip fabric, (1) elbow & knee bandage, (1) 5" x 9" Trauma Pad, (20) 3" Cotton Tipped Applicators

Dressings: (4) 3" x 3" gauze pads, (2) 4" x 4" gauze pads, (1) sterile eye pad

Medicine: (2) Ibuprofen tablets*, (2) Extra Strength Non-Aspirin Tablets*, (2) Aspirin Tablets*, (6) Burn Cream

Antiseptics: (1) Hand Sanitizer, (20) alcohol cleansing pads, (20) Antiseptic Towelettes, (1) sting relief pad, (1) Sterile Eye Wash, (6) triple antibiotic ointment packs*

These supplies should be stored in a carry-anywhere plastic case with easy carrying handle.

It is recommended that you remain abreast of the shelf-life of the medicines and ointments. These usually expire 12 months past the manufacturing date.

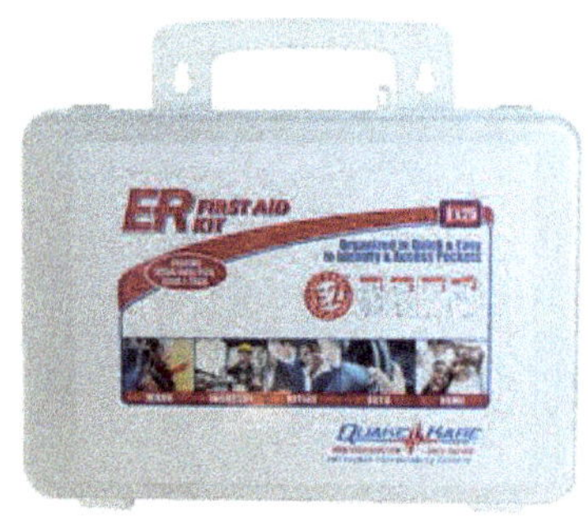

Pictured: 25 Person First Aid Kit

Trauma Central Supply Kit

This is the list for a First Aid Kit that contains comprehensive first aid items designed for disaster related and other substantial injuries for up to 75 people.

This list is as follow:
References: (1) First Aid Guide, (4) Triage Tags, (1) Scissors-EMT Surgical Shears, (1) Tweezers, (1) Forceps, (1) Scalpel Blade & Handle, (2) FDA approved Vinyl Gloves, (20) Cotton-Tipped Applicators
Injury Treatment: (4) Instant Cold Compresses, Body Warmer Pads, (2) Triangular Bandages, (5) Tongue Depressors/Splints, (5) Rolls Adhesive Tape, (25) Butterfly Closures
Bandages: (50) Adhesive 3", (2) Knuckle, (1) Fingertip, (2) Extra Large Strip
Dressings: (1) Bloodstopper Trauma Dressing, (1) Multi-Trauma 10" x 30", (5) Rolls Gauze, (12) 2" x 2" Gauze Pads, (4) 4" x 4" Gauze Pads, (4) 2" x 3" Non-Stick Pads, (4) Sterile Eye Pads
Medicines/Antiseptics: (30) Aspirin & Non-Aspirin Tablets, (50) Alcohol Prep Wipes, (10) Ammonia Inhalants, (1) Bottle Eye Wash, (1) Tube First Aid & Burn Cream, (24) Anti-Bacterial Ointment Packs, (50) Towelette Wipes, (1) Antiseptic Spray

These supplies should be stored in a water-resistant container.

It is recommended that you remain abreast of the shelf-life of the medicines and ointments. These usually expire 12 months past the manufacturing date.

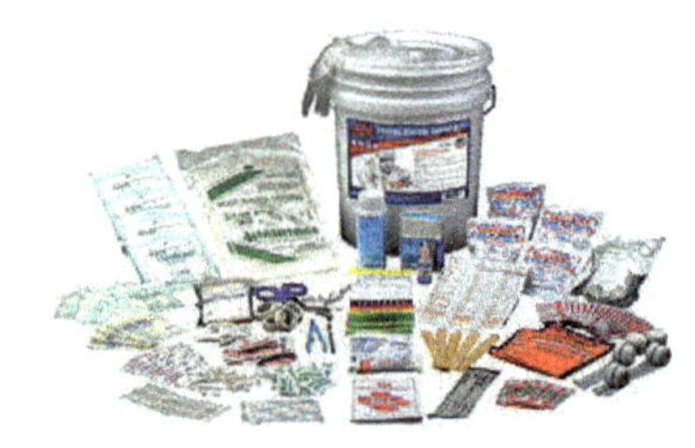

Pictured: Trauma Central Supply Kit

Medium Sized First Aid Kit

This is a list for a medium-sized First Aid Kit for your automobile, boat, or home for up to 4 people.

The list is as follows:
  (1) Durable Plastic Case
  (1) Adhesive Knuckle Fabric Bandage
  (10) Junior Adhesive Bandages, 3/8" x 1.5"
  (1) Adhesive Fingertip Fabric Bandage
  (1) Elbow Adhesive Bandage
  (10) Adhesive Bandages, ¾"x3"
  (2) Butterfly Wound Closures
  (2) Medical Grade Vinyl Gloves
  (1) Safety Pin
  (1) Triple Antibiotic Ointments*
  (4) Non-Aspirin Tablets*
  (2) Ibuprofen Tablets*
  (6) Antiseptic Towelettes
  (2) Aspirin Tablets*
  (6) Alcohol Cleansing Pads
  (1) Emergency First Aid Guide

It is recommended that you remain abreast of the shelf-life of the medicines and ointments. These usually expire 12 months past the manufacturing date.

Pictured: Medium-Sized First Aid Kit

Pet First Aid Kit

This is a list for a Pet First Aid Kit that contains emergency pet first aid items

The list is as follows:

References (1) Pet First Aid Instruction Guide
Instruments: (1) Durable zippered bag with organized compartments, (1) Scissors, (1) Tweezers, (2) Exam quality vinyl gloves, (1) oral syringe, (1) 1" x 5 yd. first aid tape roll, (12) 3" Cotton tipped applicators
Dressings: (10) 2" x 2" Gauze dressing pads, (4) 4" x 4" Gauze dressing pads, (1) 5" x 9" Trauma pad, (1) 2"x 5 yd. Wrap bandage, (2) 2" x 4.5 yd Conforming gauze roll bandage, (1) Eye Pad, (1) Triangular Bandage
Topicals: (1) Eye wash, (1) Hydrogen peroxide
Medicines & Antiseptics: (12) Antiseptic cleansing wipes, (6) Antibiotic ointment packs - Burn and Insect Relief

These supplies should be stored in a durable nylon bag.

It is recommended that you remain abreast of the shelf-life of the medicines and ointments. These usually expire 12 months past the manufacturing date.

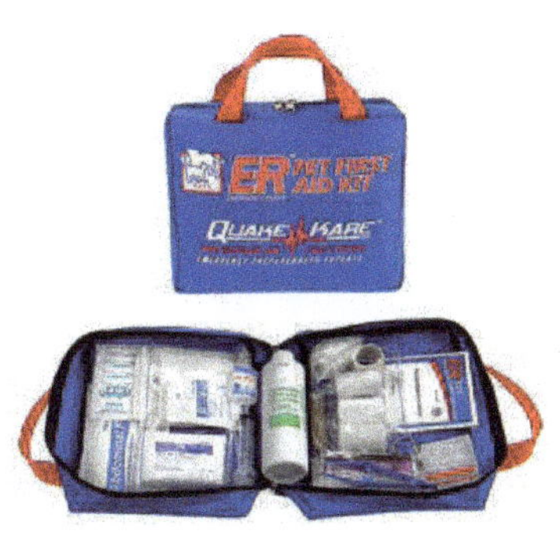

Pictured: Pet First Aid Kit

Instant Ice Pack

Ice Packs are a valuable additional to your first aid kit. Instant ice packs provide fast relief for bruises, swelling, muscle spasm, pain, headaches & minor injuries. Ice packs are a very effective and extremely easy to use first aid tool. Make sure that your Instant Ice Pack meets American National Standard - Minimum Requirements for Workplace First Aid Kits (ANSI Z308.1-1998)

This list is as follows:

(1) Instant Ice Pack

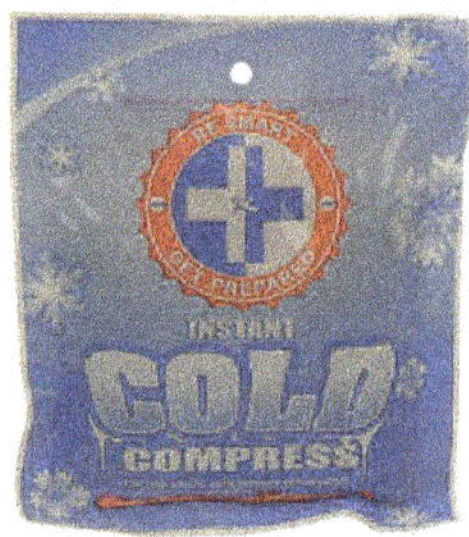

Pictured: Instant Ice Pack

CPR Mask

Emergency CPR masks offers protection from bleeding victims while administering CPR. A CPR Mask can offer effective and easy-to-use protection in the event you need to provide mouth-to-mouth resuscitation. Your CPR mask should include a large, clear vinyl shield and infection barrier for performing artificial respiration as part of cardiopulmonary resuscitation. It should be designed to protect the rescuer and the victim while aiding in the administration of the proper CPR technique, conforming easily to facial contours.

It should also be dual sided for increased effectiveness and comes with the viral and bacterial filter providing superior protection to both rescuer and victim. Other features that it should have are a positive one-way valve inside the airway to provide maximum protection of the first responder and a bite-block to assist in keeping an open airway. Utilize a CPR mask and face shield that can also be used on infants as well as small children.

Pictured: CPR Mask

CPR - Bloodborne Pathogen Kit

This is a list for an emergency CPR and bloodborne pathogen kit in order to offer protection from bleeding victims while administering CPR and first aid.

The list is as follows:

(1) CPR Mask
(1) Protective Gown
(1) Bio-hazard Bag
(1) Face Mask with Eye Shield
(1) Pair of Vinyl Gloves

Pictured: CPR - Bloodborne Pathogen Kit

Index